D0524781

Toad

By Ruth Owen

Educational Consultant:
Dee Reid

Tips for Reading with Your Child

- Set aside at least 10 to 15 minutes each day for reading.

- Find a quiet place to sit with no distractions. Turn off the TV, music and screens.

- Encourage your child to hold the book and turn the pages.

- Before reading begins, look at the pictures together and talk about what you see.

- If the reader gets stuck on a word, try reading to the end of the sentence. Often by reading the word in context, he or she will be able to figure out the unknown word. Looking at the pictures can help, too.

- Words shown in **bold** are explained in the glossary on pages 22–23.

Above all enjoy the time together and make reading fun!

Book Band Orange

For more information about toads go to: www.rubytuesdaybooks.com/wildlifewatchers

What do you know about toads?

A toad has ...
- Slimy skin
- Lumpy skin
- Spiky skin

Where does a toad live?
- In a river
- In a tree
- In a burrow

Why do toads visit ponds?
- To get a drink
- To catch fish
- To lay eggs

What is the name of a young toad?
- A toadling
- A toadlet
- A toddler

Now read this book and find the answers.

logs

It is spring in a garden.

There is a pile of logs at the end of the garden.

A toad lives under the logs in a hole called a **burrow.**

burrow

toad

Toads have lumpy skin and yellow eyes.

One evening, the toad comes out of her burrow.

The toad is going on a long walk.

She sees a fox that is hunting for small animals.

Is the toad in danger?

No.

When the fox was younger it tried to eat a toad and the toad tasted horrible!

That is because a toad's skin makes **poison**.

Now the fox knows not to eat the toad and it runs away.

The toad walks out of the garden and into a field.

A grass snake slithers towards her.

Is the toad in danger?

No.

The toad puffs up her body until she is as big as a tennis ball!

The snake thinks the toad is too big to eat and it slithers away.

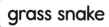
grass snake

The toad walks all evening until it gets dark.

She walks onto a road.

A car is coming towards her!

Is the toad in danger?

No.

There is a sign on the road to tell people that toads may be crossing.

The car slows down to let the toad cross the road.

Where is the toad going?

She is walking towards a large pond.

In spring, lots of toads meet up
in ponds to **mate**.

The toad jumps into the pond and
mates with a male toad.

She lays about 5000 tiny eggs under the water.

The eggs are in long strings.

strings of eggs

When she has laid her eggs, the toad walks all the way back to the garden.

tadpoles

After about 10 days, tiny **tadpoles** hatch from the toad's eggs.

The tadpoles have long tails.

Soon the tadpoles grow back legs.

toad tadpole

Then the tadpoles grow front legs.

Their tails get shorter and shorter.

When the tadpoles are about eight weeks old they climb out of the pond.

Now they are called toadlets.

Each tiny toadlet will find a little hole to be its burrow.

After about four years, each toadlet will become an adult toad.

A scientist holding a toadlet.

What has the mother toad been doing all summer?

All day she stays in her burrow.

worm

At night she hunts for worms, snails, slugs and **insects**.

snail

slug

She catches them
with her long,
sticky tongue.

When autumn comes, the weather gets cold.

The toad goes into her burrow under the pile of logs.

She stays there all winter and does not go outside.

Soon it will be spring, and time to walk to the pond to lay more eggs!

Glossary

burrow
A hole or tunnel that an animal digs as a home.

insect
A small animal with six legs and a body in three parts.

mate
To get together to produce young.

poison
A substance that is harmful to people and animals. A toad's body produces poison. This helps protect the toad from animals that want to eat it.

tadpole
A young frog or toad that has a long tail and lives in water.

Toad Quiz

1 Why didn't the fox eat the toad?

2 How did the toad stay safe from the snake?

3 How many eggs did the toad lay in the pond?

4 How is a tadpole different from a toadlet?

5 What foods does a toad eat?

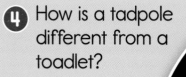